This book was made

for birds that hum

and eagles high above.

To give them words

and raise a voice

to save their sounds we love.

To Kersti + Bey

ISBN 978-1-7352102-5-4
All rights reserved. First hardcover edition, February 2025.
Visit kocreatebooks.com for permission requests and more information.

Special thanks to Kersti Muul, a tireless advocate, researcher, rescuer, activist, and voice for birds and wildlife in the urban world we share. Her stories and efforts have inspired West Seattle and this book.

Story, design & illustrations
©2025 Lori Kothe

kocreatebooks.com

Birds
Near My Home
IN THE CITY BY THE SEA

Lori Kothe

gulp.

caw! caw! caw! caw!

swoooosh!

Deet de de de de deet

screeech!

bzz bzz bzz bzz

ha! ha!

ha!
ha!

HONK! HONK! HONK!

Who hoo   hoo hooot!

Near my home

in the city by the sea,

birds soar and swim

and speak to me.

Eagles and seagulls,

owls, herons, and jays,

falcons, crows, hummers,

and geese go their ways.

Bald Eagle
Haliaeetus leucocephalus

Deet de de de de deet de de de deet!

Deet de de de de deet de de de deet!

"Deet-de-de-de-de-deet-de-de-de-deet!"

Look up in that tree!

It's a Bald Eagle pair.

So mighty and massive,

one takes to the air.

Searching for dinner,

or a maybe a fight,

that's one bird that makes my cat

tremble in fright.

Bey is a beloved Bald Eagle who lives in West Seattle. Wildlife biologist Kersti Muul matched photos of an anomaly in Bey's left iris to identify her after a rescue. The Bald Eagle wasn't officially designated as the national bird of the United States until 2024!

explore: paws.org

Glaucous-Winged Gull
Larus glaucescens

"Ha-ha-ha-ha!"

The seagulls all laugh

when you visit the beach

knowing a picnic

will soon be in reach.

They smile and watch

and they circle the skies

ready to swoop down

and eat up your fries.

A statue of Ivar feeding French fries to seagulls can be found on the Seattle waterfront near the iconic local restaurant *Ivar's Acres of Clams*. When a gull catches a hard-shell creature like an oyster, it flies high up in the air and drops it to break it open.

explore: eopugetsound.org

Great Horned Owl
Bubo virginianus

Who hoo hoo hooot!

Who hooo hoo hooot!

"Who-hooo-hoo-hooot!"

A Great Horned Owl HOOT

wakes me in my bed.

I think of how it hunts at night

and turns around its head.

Sometimes it's called a tiger owl

or hoot owl when it cries.

It sees much better in the dark

with big, bold yellow eyes.

Adult Great Horned Owls sometimes get injured when they attack prey, including being stuck with porcupine quills and sprayed by skunks! You can protect owls from poison by avoiding the use of rodenticide and pesticide in your yard.

explore: sarveywildlife.org

Great Blue Heron
Ardea herodias

gulp.

"Roh-roh-roh. STAB! Gulp. Gulp."

There stands a Blue Heron

as still as a stone.

So quiet and peaceful

and happy alone.

It's ever so slender

but surely not weak.

Just ask the poor fish

that it stabbed with its beak!

In 2003, Seattle named the Great Blue Heron as the official City Bird after it won a public contest. Great Blue Herons can be seen courting and nesting from February to August at Commodore Park and other colonies in the Seattle area.

explore: heronhelpers.org

Steller's Jay

Cyanocitta stelleri

"Screech-screech-screech-screech!
Shack-shack-shack!"

The blue Steller's Jay

is so noisy and bold,

it is no wonder

a group's called a scold.

What mimics a squirrel sound

and acts like a brat?

That food-robbing bird

with the fancy black hat.

> The very vocal Steller's Jay and Steller Sea Lion are both West Coast natives named for Georg Steller, a German naturalist and explorer. Steller's Jays can imitate the sounds of birds, squirrels, cats, dogs, chickens, and even mechanical objects.
>
> explore: allaboutbirds.org

Peregrine Falcon
Falco peregrinus

SWOOOOOSH!

"Flap-flap-flap. SWOOOSH!"

The Peregrine Falcon

is fastest of all.

Some nest on a building

800 feet tall!

Stoop is the word

for its dive from so high

to catch prey in mid-air

right out of the sky.

The Peregrine Falcon is the fastest flying bird in the world and can exceed 200 mph in a dive. Peregrines have famously nested on a Seattle skyscraper ledge since 1994. You can watch new fledglings grow up each year via online Seattle Falcon Cams!

explore: urbanraptorconservancy.org

Crow

Corvus brachyrhynchos / Corvus caurinus

caw! caw! caw! caw!

caw! caw! caw! caw!

caw! caw! caw! caw!

"Caw-caw-caw-caw! Caw!"

Every so often

the crows call a meeting.

Hundreds arrive

and they CAW with a greeting.

They come to the tree

that's the tallest in sight.

What do they say

as they banter in flight?

> Nearly 16,000 crows fly in at dusk each evening to roost at a restored wetland near UW Bothell, about 20 miles northeast of Seattle. But not all crows go to Bothell. Many Seattle crows go southeast and hang out near the mall at a large roost in Renton.
>
> **explore: uwb.edu/visitors/crows**

Anna's Hummingbird
Calypte anna

bzz bzz bzz bzz

humm humm

"Bzz-bzz-bzz-bzz. Humm humm."

Fall and winter,

summer and spring,

Anna's Hummingbird

doesn't sing.

It hums instead

like a hovering bee –

an iridescent dragonfly

floating magically.

Hummingbirds are the smallest migrating bird, with over 330 known species in North and South America. Of the four species found in Washington State, only the Anna's Hummingbird stays home in winter to brighten Seattle year-round.

explore: birdsconnectsea.org

Canada Goose
Branta canadensis

"HONK HONK HONK! Hiss. Hiss."

The Canada Goose

is a sight to see

when up in the sky

you notice a V.

But be sure to look down

to see where it's gone

or you might step in goose poop

that's left on the lawn.

A Canada Goose can poop every 12 minutes and produce up to three pounds of poop per day! Goose poop contains bacteria that can make people sick and contaminate water. You can help by not feeding geese when you visit a local park, lake, or shoreline.

explore: wa.audubon.org

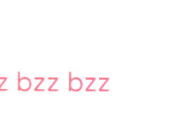

Now I know

in the city by the sea,

it's home to birds

and not just me.

They make it such a special place

to live and grow and share.

I love to listen to their calls

across the land and air.

Help birds at home

Want to create a better home for wild birds where you live?
It's easy! You don't even need a birdhouse or a big backyard. A few changes to the outdoor space around you can make a big difference for birds and people alike.

A healthy wildlife habitat requires food, water, shelter, and safe space. What's missing from your yard, neighborhood, or region? What can you do? The checklist to the right is a good starting point for ideas. Then explore local and online resources for expert guidance in your area.

If you live in Washington State, check out the "Habitat at Home" program that helps people learn ways to connect with nature, increase biodiversity, coexist with wildlife, and foster healthier, happier communities. You can even receive a sign to put in your yard to recognize your wildlife habitat and inspire others!

wdfw.wa.gov/species-habitats/living/habitat-at-home

WILDLIFE HABITAT CHECKLIST

 ### Food
- Native plants with seeds, nuts, or berries
- Clean and safe bird feeders

 ### Water
- Shallow baths with gradual sloped sides
- Bird baths or water containers regularly cleaned to protect birds from disease

 ### Shelter
- Trees, shrubs, and ground cover
- Leaves and dead trees/snags
- Grass or brush cuttings for nest building

 ### Safe space
- No pesticides or rodent poisons
- Natural yard care practices to keep soil, air, and water healthy
- Protection from cats, dogs, and predators

 ### You!
Be a voice that gets your human neighbors excited and interested in how they can help birds, too!

About the author/illustrator

Lori Kothe is a purpose-driven author, designer, and founder who has called Seattle home since 1996. She lives with her family near Alki Beach in West Seattle where eagles and seagulls, owls, herons, and jays, falcons, crows, hummers, and geese go their ways.

gulp.

swooooosh!

screeech!

bzz bzz bzz bzz

caw! caw! caw! caw!

ha!
ha!
ha!
ha!

Deet de de de de deet

HONK! HONK! HONK!

Who hoo   **hoo hooot!**

www.ingramcontent.com/pod-product-compliance
Lightning Source LLC
LaVergne TN
LVRC090147080526
838200LV00093B/369